e Praise for Binary Stars

"In her debut collection *Binary Stars*, Dana Koster bravely scouts the fierce, alien, and surprisingly dangerous landscapes of family life and relationships. From the epigraph, 'The Moon Smells Like Burnt Gunpowder,' we are situated in alien territory where even 'the molecules… [are] all wrong.' From this sense of displacement, Koster writes—with spare and tender language—of the wild, fairy tale nature of the domestic everyday, where a father resembles a werewolf, where mothers perceive their infants as parasitic grotesques. In this extraordinary first book, lovers, mothers, children and siblings are inextricably linked to one another and, just like binary stars, they threaten to destroy each other, as well. Koster's dark humor becomes the dark matter imbuing her poetic cosmos, which 'fills/the gaps/in the night/with seeming.'; dark matter is the medium by which ghosts, living and not, haunt this collection." —STELLA BERATLIS

"Dana Koster's *Binary Stars* reminds us that we don't journey in a straight line through life: we revolve, through day and night, through season, and most importantly, through our human relationships. Her sharp, funny, dark poems chart long orbits, and to move with them—from the mousewife to motherhood to earwigs to dark matter—is to travel from illumination to illumination." —MARIA HUMMEL

"We need a new word (astro-tropism?) for the poetry of *Binary Stars*. For the way it leaps into stellar depths to cast a gaze sharp as a hummingbird's beak back on the extended family cluster. Two stars, a larger and a smaller, in tight rotation, yield binary poems in clumps and couplets in the first person dual and second person singular: to the baby, the husband (with orbiting cows, horses, and almonds), the burned out but still gravitational father-in-law and mother, and the therapist, whose analytical gaze is returned with equal intensity. Koster has written a domestic poetry not 'of the heart,' not soft-focused, but of the barycenter, the binary center of gravity, in which the familiar, thrown off kilter, becomes alienated, estranged, and new. Dare you read a poetry at the white heat? Then open *Binary Stars*, an incandescent book of the first magnitude." —JOHN SHOPTAW

binary stars

Dana Koster

Poetry Series #20
CAROLINA WREN PRESS
Durham, North Carolina

Series Editor: Andrea Selch
Title Editor: David Kellogg
Design: Lesley Landis Designs

Cover Image:
©2015 North American Nebula
AstroWimp/Tim Christensen

Author Photograph:
©2016 Photos Just So

The mission of Carolina Wren Press is to seek out, nurture and promote literary work by new and underrepresented writers, including women and writers of color.

Carolina Wren Press is a 501(c)3 nonprofit organization supported in part by grants and generous individual donors. This publication was made possible by ongoing support made possible through gifts to the Durham Arts Council's United Arts Fund.

Library of Congress Cataloging-in-Publication Data

Names: Koster, Dana, 1983- author
Title: Binary stars / Dana Koster.
Description: Durham, North Carolina : Carolina Wren Press, [2017] |
Series:
Carolina Wren Press poetry series ; 20
Identifiers: LCCN 2016050855 | ISBN 9780932112804 (pbk.)
Classification: LCC PS3611.O7492365 A6 2017 | DDC 811/.6--dc23
LC record available at https://lccn.loc.gov/2016050855

for justin

Contents

The Moon Smells Like Burnt Gunpowder

How did we smell it when our heads were screwed
into our helmets? Easy. We touched it

with gloved hands, walked the empty vistas
like shades of the Otherworld,

and the regolith held an electric charge,
stuck to everything: the crannies

of our suits, the Module's disced feet—
a fine film of lunar soil

that filled the cabin with the smell
of bitter sulfur, Roman candles

aimed at a best friend's ear.
Made you feel the red prickles of a kickbruise

welling on your shoulder, back when
the moon was a faraway dream.

But when we studied the molecules,
they were all wrong—not combustible at all.

Just glass. Motes formed
and scattered by meteorite impacts.

The moon smells like burnt gunpowder,
we said. We had to say something.

ONE

Discovery

I woke, as I tend to, with stars
crumbing my eyes. There was dark.
Nights took longer to observe.

I roved the house in search of you
and found water, instead. Some few signs of life:
a displaced coffee pot, a voice I mistook for yours
wraithing the radio.

It could have been me
who displaced, who repeated
albedo, albedo until the lights dimmed.

Discovery: a year depends upon your orbit.
Small impacts are never small—will ripple
even the stillest surface.

Hummingbird Heart

Little one, they say five hummingbird chicks
fit in a teaspoon, that adults
impale one another with their beaks,
right through the chest. For nectar, for
shelter. For no small thing.

What comes next is beyond guesswork,
beyond gene charts or sonograms. Already
you would fit in a pint—soon a quart,
a gallon, a bread box. Not even a chirp
from you yet and already I know:
what I would do for you
I could not name.

As long as you're in there,
I have two hearts. This old standard
that rattles my chest and yours—
swooping across the monitor,
little flutter on the screen.

Nesting

When you are born I will say: love me
as I loved my own mother—desperately,
as though love could stitch a path to the dead

and I will guard you with the greed of ancestry.
Oh Starling, Magpie, my Dove
I'll never eat eggs again, I'll slaughter
snakes and foxes, I'll build a house of reeds.

I'll age one year for each question
you ask of me, small one, so choose well
and cradle the answers in the shell of your ear.

Sonnet Among the Almond Trees

Half-standing on the tractor, half-sitting in Justin's lap,
I weave left, right, duck down to avoid a face of pink-
blossomed branches. His hand reaches across my back,
steadies me, and I am expansive, just on the brink
of becoming the figurehead of a John Deere.
I'm losing her, he says. *You have to help me steer,*
and I do, but the tractor lurches to the right with a groan,
then stops. We laugh, our voices merging with the drone
of forty bee hives at farm's edge. Undeterred, we gun it hard,
put it in second and rush forward like the flock
of chickens we chased yesterday in the yard.
Marriage is like this: a fruitful machine, sudden starts and stops,
and always the knowledge that somewhere your father
knows what you are doing and disapproves.

Yellow Window

When we touch, I hear the rumble of horses.
I'd forgotten the pasture is full of horses.

In sleep, you entice me to swallow your breath.
I will not break you as one breaks horses.

Outside, the earth is flat and resolute.
Fog rolls through the valley on the backs of horses.

I wonder if I will outlive you, or you me,
but I only ask you to speak of horses.

You say there are filaments of night in my hair.
I am telling you they are strands of horseness.

The moon is not a spy at our yellow window.
The sun is not a chariot pulled by horses.

The Wolf at the Door

Your father says you've all got a bit of the werewolf
in you and continues shoveling. He drawls the word *werewolf*

until I swear I see it arc out from his lips—or else
the heat is playing tricks on me. Turning pumpkin seeds to wolf's

teeth. Sweat curls the hairs on your neck as you rupture the earth
beside him, ignoring our conversation, the lone wolf,

as always. I try to see the beast rippling beneath the skin
of this old man, but the wrong celestial body bears down on us. Wolves

need moonlight like these rows need water. Like your father needs to
disappear from the house. And before, I never thought *werewolf*

when he would irrigate at dusk, but now the image of his pelt
reflected in those flooded fields comes unbidden. The wolf

in him calling to coyotes in the distance, flaring with
the temper you remember from childhood, when the wolf

could hardly be kept from the door. But your own temper comes only
as a snarl and you turn away from me—docile as you ever were.

Fiddlehead

Inside the gnarled green spire
I see our son's eyes: sporeling

-to-be, no more than a seed among
myriad seeds in a portrait

of our own eyes. Blink, and he shivers
into being, nothing like we portrayed

him. So often what we imagine
fractures this way, as porcelain.

In the garden, fiddlehead remains
between us: budding, waiting to spore.

We stare at the coiled frond, poised for its
unfurling—whatever that portends.

Ice Plant

I confide: sand will be sufficient. Rocks.
You'll root easily, hardly desire
water—take only the necessities,
cuttings.

Love is all. Love, and you're golden.
Have that, and you won't fuck up
this baby, you won't avoid your spouse's eyes
over brunch. You'll brunch.
Squalling nighttime wakings
won't change you.

I flatter. I lie.
You are glowing,
I purr, like uranium glass
under a blacklight—
trace amounts
permeate all you touch.

Changeling

if I put scissors above his   cradle
or swaddled him   with keys   if

sweating and staining the blankets its face
pinched echo of his face it is an   abstract
  rushed summary in the mornings   I look
   into its mouth and

we don't have a name for   this anymore
      we've lost it   we've lost it

who could nurse
   that awful   smile clamped
      jaw   suckling suckling

refuse
to follow
                procedure   to touch
                   to feed

                         the things
      I've lost sit
                      on   the shelves
                              howling
                      the
                things
                      I've
         lost
                      dwindle
into
         smoke

Binary Stars

I.

In the moment of upsuck, quiet eye
of the storm that was your mouth
gawping open
                in another
                              endless howl
I thought every tender part of me
had broken. Replaced with
        something wild
that even then
would not let me
set you down.

Westley. I speak your name here
so you will know me
in your first months:
shade of myself. Flickering
in and out of view.

I didn't want a daughter, only
a son. I could never wish this on you.

II.

A flurry of red hairs
pooled in the drain—
what remained
of my loveliness
sloughing off,
a death knell.

It was not
the first time
my hair fell
free of me.
For years after
your grandmother died
I pulled it out.

When you were
four weeks old,
I cried in a salon.
Told the hairdresser:
cut it all off.

III.

At 11:53 that horrible nurse
dumped you on my chest.
Westley, my firstborn boy,
      I saw
      I'd given birth
      to a small stranger.

A stocky thing
      with my eyes,
blue-tinged and mewling.

I could feel   all the anger
go into me, could calmly
flay a man
for not supporting your head.

IV.

I was selfish. I wished you to look
like Justin:
a thatch
of dark hair,
kissable
mole under
black lashes.

Or my mother, thin-
lipped and slim, blonde
                    tendrils of her
                            born back.

But the features you drew from me
were all my father:
elfin ears that stick out
at the tip, double-cowlick,
even the twice-jointed thumbs
that scared us at first.
My father, who never called:
you wore him like a curse.
Even your eyes
are really his
                    staring strangely,
a mirror within a mirror
spiraling through history.

V.

There were times I was primordial, barely
lifting us two from the slime, the muck,
tripping from couch to kitchen
and back.   Trapped
    and hopeless,
            buckling
suction tubes to my breasts.

Human, animal, extraterrestrial—
how does any life exist?
How have any mothers
done this
before me?
Love is something you and I
have stumbled on, Westley.
A disease that needed time
to gestate. We just are.
Impossibly loud, skin
to skin—binary stars.

Mousewife

She cooks and cleans and bites
her tongue. Then, at night,
she eats her young.

TWO

Pathfinder

We bound ourselves
to other minerals.
Pretended
we were water.

I became
an invader, twisted
in the wreckage
of my body.

You tried
distraction.
Transmuted
magma to basalt

but our shelter
was temporary.

Foreign objects
were only pieces
of ourselves
we had forgotten.

Remote, the pink sky
glinted. Escape
as unattainable
as oxygen.

The Firefighter's Wife

She itched to light
her first cigarette in years,
to take a good drag and flick

that bright cherry of ash
onto the dry brush
of their backyard.

Anything to bring him back
from someone else's home.
On the news,

helicopters dropped
their wet cargo
on the ecstatic hills

while the winds thrilled
at shifting, gifting the landscape
this unexpected purge.

The fire line broke.
All the sane animals fled
at the first sign of smoke.

The Earwig

Down in the mud she hollows a grotto no bigger
than an ear, lays her eggs in the darkness and quivers
over them, incessantly circling her clutch
until my spade descends to scatter the nest.
I want to take her doting as a lesson, remember
the way her pincers repulse me even as she uses them
to carry her young, fastidiously cleaning each one
of fungi and the strangeness I exposed them to.
In seven days, the nymphs will emerge translucent
and horrible, molting darker and larger with each instar,
devouring the food she regurgitates: my wisteria
and red lettuce, the dahlias I raise and stake each year.
And if I am generous, in the spirit of motherhood,
I will leave them all for the chickens.

Murmuration

The crocodile fat in her man suit,
clicking her teeth with a hook—
too big for this skin. Her jaws unfurl
into a snaggled maw with every grin.

Uncomely. Ready
to slit Pan's belly, gobble
the world whole.

Hungry for the legions
of shadow children
trailing the boat.

Dancing, the lost boys murmur,
is the opposite of cringe.

Clocks we couldn't help but swallow
tick tick ticking deep within.

Combustion

I am thick as a candle
freshly dipped—this
tallow and flesh
are wax; my dress
is a wick
of human
ignition.

These bones will smolder
beyond recognition.

The Head is a Canvas

These are the things we keep hidden: our bodies when we cannot bear
them. Our lenient stomachs. Our shame. We are gifted bearers.

Last night, you exposed your scalp: no hair to hide behind, black whorls
on the skin. *The head is a canvas*, you said, your teeth bared.

I held so many nothings on my tongue. I wanted to say:
How much the hair has changed you. How much we refuse to bare.

You thought these were your choices: red wig or brown. Thick hips or
cocaine. We falter in this climate. We lose our bearings.

Even when the sky is heat-muted cornflower. Even when
nectarines plump and languish on the branch, we search for bareness.

Coyote

Coyote followed me
to my car, followed me
past the tumbleweeds, past
the wagon wheel splayed
like a heart in the desert
weeds—cooing *baby, sweet
thing*, circling to my back. Said he knows
a place we can be alone. Said he wants
to tell me a story.

I'd heard about this one's long
tail, his quick tongue, and I said
he'd best shut his mouth
so I could drive.

What if he took me
beneath the water tower
and never said a word? What if
I rode him hard in the backseat
of that sedan, or hooked my boots
over his shoulders, told him
to lick each one, heel to tip?
Coyote, I can make
my own stories, will make
and make long after you've run dry.

Mama warned of those that bite:
mosquito, rattler, coyote.
Mama, be damned. Your daughters
all got teeth, too.

Coming Home

Unpeaced, unhorsed, we enter into the covenant
of peach trees. Is our blossom breath uncovered?

Cow pushed through barbed wire to get outside—
we try to guide him back. He runs from cover.

Won't stop chasing him long enough to put
shoes on. In our feet, oat kernels dig tiny coves.

No way to surround him, no way to tempt
him back. We are helpless in the clover.

Some would rather a bullet between the eyes
than a trip home. Cow runs his hooves cloven.

Nautilus

It's hardly about forgiveness. His cock
shrivels with memory, the kiss
disappears—and this
is what no one tells you: it's forgetting
that makes a marriage stick.

Maybe the recoil
is a temporary retreat,
necessary withdrawal
to smaller chambers.

Or maybe we'll barter our fingers
for dozens of ribbed tentacles
and never lose our grip. Who's to say?
Every day we are unfaithful
in some new way.

Gobsmacked

I remember you then, barely old enough
to grow a beard, gobsmacked
by ease of conversation.
The night we peeled oranges
in that cramped kitchen until morning;
didn't dare touch
for fear
of what came next.

So many nights since then
I've leaned into your body—
to brush my cheek across the black hairs
on your shoulders, to feel
your familiar heaviness within.

Outside, the sweet
rancidity of the tallow plant
hangs in the air. How many years
have we searched this flat horizon
for something more, some sign
of a mountain pass? Already
I can barely trace
the small measures
that have led us here. Already
I wonder how much longer
this can go on.

Star Map

This one in the rudimentary shape
of a man: his abrupt limbs
ending. The space
between the man
and the forked tongue
at his shoulder
always expanding.

THREE

Endeavour

A speck amongst specks—
a shadow against the mesosphere,

always on your way
to somewhere else.

All that you mended and assembled
remembers your touch.

How you turned a room
weightless with your bearing.

Kablooey

Ghazal for America

The man on the TV says someone we love is always dying
but he's wrong—everyone we love is always dying

and what's more I tell him what's more is that miracle vial
you're searching for won't fix a goddamned thing. Diane

I tell him though that's not his name Diane no elixir will
grow back your ladyfriend's skin. It's kablooey. It was dynamite

back in the day but now it's something off the butcher's block
and I'm sorry darling but she's kaput. Times are dire

and if I lost a leg outside the green zone you'd tell me
the same thing. Maybe you're more a *diamond*

is half full sort of guy I don't know—I've never been
much of an optometrist. Chances are we won't be dining

this way again so I'd like to say before you sign off:
expletive deleted. You're a real pal a dynamo

in the sack but don't fool yourself. We're only watching
because those folks on the other channels are always dying

to sell us five-in-one pasta strainers and knives that cut through
tomatoes. But really don't all knives cut through tomatoes Diane?

Griefbook

Our grief is cloud
computed. Crowd-
sourced, transmuted
to text and screen.
It wants to know
if he was sick.
If he didn't
hit his head,
why so much blood?
It needs to know
how he is dead.

Our grief needs emoticons,
it needs multitudes of <3s
and RIPs. Platitudes
superimposed over pictures
of the grey salt sea.

Our grief blows up my phone
with messages, calls, photos
of his sparse beard
and awful ties. A litany
of broad goodbyes—
ex-lovers, those
he barely knew
or met in bars
"need clarity."

Our grief tags him anew—
it doesn't want
to believe this.
Our grief writes
Brother, Friend
into the ether
and pretends that
wherever he is,
he can read it.

We Went Back to Get Your Checkbook

And what did I expect—a chalk outline?
A cold rush of air?

We found only evidence of his life.
Nothing of what comes after.

*

Your propensity for beauty betrayed you.
Luminous curtains trapped the sunlight,
retched it onto every surface of the room.
Rick would love this inverted trope—
in movies, after all,
it's always raining at a funeral.
On the day of his, my thighs
heat-bonded to the pew.

He would have wanted
to break with tradition, I offered.

You searched the shelves
for his last book recommendation.

He wouldn't want to be dead.

*

There was no one to shift the colors
towards blue in post-processing. No one
to adjust the lights, to ensure your face
was side lit, hardened by shadow.
It was just your darling apartment:
your converted-water-tower-loft

stuck through with a spiral staircase,
overhung by soaring redwood beams.

Sun-gilded, a mason jar with dregs
of ginger tea sat on the counter
where he left it, and in this way,
every mundane artifact
shone warm and glorious—
even the sprouted potato
he was trying to cultivate, that he swore
he would plant.

*

He sat on that couch
and took off his shoes.

Those red tennis shoes
belong to a dead person.

*

*Rick died. He died
and he is dead.*

I want to conjugate
a way out of this,
a future for you,
but the tense
changes nothing.

He died.
He will be dead.

*

At first, we both kept slipping up,
speaking in present tense.

But he has so many plans,
you told me. *And orange specks*
in his eyes.

You found him there
on the hardwood floor,
too rigid to resuscitate.
The shower still running.

His hair is soft and fine and really thick.

How can he change my life like this
and not be here to live it with me?

*

You wore the same striped polo shirt
all week, so I sifted through your vintage floral
hook-and-eye dresses,
the drawers of lacy underthings.

    On a double date, we all agreed
    you would be played by Zooey Deschanel
    for wardrobe alone. It was an obvious choice.
    We had assumed it
    was a romantic comedy—
    Rick would be played
    by Bradley Cooper in cargo shorts
    and wrestling tees. We drank too much.
    He called the casting generous
    and seemed pleased.

    *

We will all be dead people,
you say.

I edge us towards dramedy:
That would make a great
album name.

You're right, though, of course.

*

I picked you a simple nude bra
and three work-appropriate cardigans.
Thought your role more appropriate, now,
for Jennifer Lawrence.

*

You went to the bathroom last.
The police didn't clean up the blood
but Martin brought rubber gloves,
scrubbed the stained porcelain
before we arrived.

*

The night Rick died
there were so many shoes
scuffing the floors, displacing laundry—
the house was a wreck.

His toothbrush is the green one.
Again, the tense all wrong.
The faint bleach smell
out of place.

The stars we cast in your biopic
are already practicing
the motion: trying
and failing
to pick up a toothbrush
and throw it out.

Axiom

This was the axiom: she would succumb
to cancer. They were to help her wring from
life what joy they could—pour her brandy
and cajole: if this makes her happy,
it doesn't hurt. Fear became the theorem

of the house, a rule deduced from tantrums
she threw over dishes, length of denim
skirts. Slights real and imagined. Maybe
this was the axiom:

there is no cure, no hope of remission.
But she lives—leaves bottles of Ketel One
half-drunk in closets, stashed in laundry.
The mind is stronger than the body.
We can know how a life will be undone—
was this the axiom?

Scouting

When the girls search for birds they find only owl
pellets, tight balls of bone they bury with trowels.

A dutiful concealment, this childhood
of funerals: the ecstatic and the foul.

Bees that stung them moments before
entombed in a shoebox, shrouded in towels.

They uncover what it means to bury,
if what fills the shovel suppresses the howl.

Emergency Response

Our evenings were Domino's pizza and carrot sticks,
my brother pleading for one last round of Super Mario

before bed. Afterwards, we'd scale the top bunk
like mountaineers, race to stick our gum to the bedposts.

And if the phone rang out, if a babysitter warmed the couch
while we slept, we never heard it—our mother stealing

from the apartment, ashing one last cigarette
out the window of the station wagon

before she climbed the stairs to some other child's hell.
After her funeral, I found the details in newspaper clippings:

a woman and son spotted through two-way glass,
her fist wadded tight around his shirt collar;

urine-soaked mattresses; infants with their bones split.
And I remembered braiding the yarn hair of a doll

in her office, then removing its dress—the thrill
of discovering all the parts Barbie was missing.

Ceremony

it was a child's harebrained scheme and we knew it
but he said   *let's start a fire*
while he teased the black cats
in his pocket

so I whispered *I'm in*
and the firecrackers streamed from his corduroys
     like a magician's handkerchief

we dug the pit without instrument
lugged together   fence parts   pylons
for our rigged-up cross-ditch

and our shadows
strobed the sanddrifts
with every shank of wood
we threw on the blaze

all for the phrase:
          if your mother
               could see you now
          she'd turn over in her grave

We Do Not Speak

I scratch wax from the underbelly of the table. What
is there to say? You do not want to be here—what

we want so rarely matters in this world. Neither of us will
speak about your roommate, whose life you saved last night. What

you told the nurses was not *George has stopped breathing* but
George has gone to meet his family. Somehow they knew what

you meant. Here, everyone wears a robe and slippers,
a farce of Sunday mornings where even what

you wear could kill you. Sneakers are forbidden—a shoelace might
as well be a noose. Brother, take my hand. I want to ask what

ghosts you see when your eyes are open and if you'll meet your
family, too. If our mother haunts this place, or if the ghost is you.

Arson Poetica

I've memorized the distance from
finger to forehead, I've struck
the match head, I'm deciding
which letters to burn. Dear Virginia,
we are all complicit, Santa never existed
outside of your bed. Dear Witches, I've
yearned for your taloned kisses, I too
have been spurned by the tales of men.

Dear all of the women I've wronged,
who have wronged me, Dear Daughter,
Dear Sister, Dear Auntie, Dear Friend,
I've always loved you, I'm sorry, bear
with me, I'm torching the fences
inside of my head.

Dear Mama, I waited, I suffered, I fevered
but your ghost was unruly, you never
appeared. And if you were there cousins
and night birds and lovers, why can't I
remember the things that you said?

Cinderella, your gown is caught
at your ankles, you should have
been cared for. Your mother is dead.

Ghazal for Aurora Chasing the Deer

Maybe it's that you asked first, that such simple courtesy is gone
as soon as you take off after the deer. One step and you've gone

feral, no impish child flitting towards woodland friend but
a glimpse of what we all are underneath: predators or goners.

Only twelve, and already this village can barely contain you,
can barely keep you from slitting the doe's throat, let alone goad

you into something civilized. Still, you've discovered that
asking for permission rather than forgiveness can gain

you both. May you tackle the deer to their knees, Aurora,
and may you never stop, not even when you've grown,

not even when your russet hair has crept to grey.
You must be the one who feeds when the rest of us are gone.

FOUR

Moon Dogs

Puffs of ice in your atmosphere tilt light
into a ring. Tonight I am on your surface,
watching the clouds bestow on our son

his own halo, two bright obscurities:
pale siblings that spark the circle's edges.
Our little moon refracted into moons unreal—

a wonder, once gone, we won't see again.
What the ice gives, it takes away.
We three left to blink out, one by one.

Pallbearing

We hold hands during the service because there is no other place
for hands. Every part of us is clumsy in this room, pallid

and unbelieving. The minister raps about Lazarus,
who rose from the dead after four days, lit up a Pall

Mall and swaggered out of his tomb—Jesus saves us all, they
say, in less obvious ways. Your grandfather lies pale

beside the pulpit, makes no move to stand. I lock arms
with my sister-in-law and prepare to watch you, pallbearers,

brothers hefting your forefather's coffin from the hearse.
Jennifer confides she doesn't envy a man's place

in these ceremonies (grief on display, arms straining to bear
the weight), but tasks can be a luxury. Can placate

our bones. If we lift with the legs, take these small steps forward,
maybe we'll believe this is all according to plan.

Guinevere

"Better that Guinevere had been
drowned at birth," Merlin said,
but there's a certain joy
in witnessing the end of something good,
in laying to rest a favorite doll
after overuse.

Seven Nights Without Ghosts

I. THE CHAIR

Tell them about the rocking chair that appeared
at her wake. Crate seven feet tall, Wink and Jeff
dismantling the monument with hands, knives, anything
within reach.

Tell them about the violets
tangling the seat of it, how you ran
your fingers over needlepoint petals,
willed it to move.

Gosling, if your mother
only knew, her heart
would surely break
in two.

II. STORYBOOK

Remember the Goose Girl?
Her mother's blood flecked
a handkerchief, spoke
when spoken to, was lost
forever in the river. Perhaps
your prayers have gone
that route, too.

III. HALLWAY

That first night, you saw a light
under the door.

The hallway was dark
and closed at both ends.

IV. CORNERS

In a song against heaven
you crushed the mouths
of strays you attracted.
Surely, you thought,
spirits or seraphs will crawl
from these wounds.

V. WALLS

Still she didn't.
Not in dreams
or doorways,
though you
peered through the veil,
listened with your bones.

Just a trick
of the pipes,
that wheezing
in the walls.

That owl
on the threshold—
an idle bird.

VI. NIGHT TERROR

Your husband tells you later that he couldn't
wake you, that you keened
in your sleep, whimpered for her—

what he wouldn't give
for a Visitation, to know
which brick to bury
under what moon.

VII. NURSERY

You've known as many nights without
as with, have conducted
your own warbling baby
into the world.

Perhaps she straightens her picture,
rocks the embroidered chair
when you leave the room

and you are the presence
in the hallway who flickers
the lights, continuously
summoned back
into the witching hour.

Separate Beds

That most nights I can't sleep without you
sequestered in another room, your mouth
slung open like that dead cow

in the meadow—its indecently erect legs
tilted to the moon—means what, exactly?
That your snores hum to me

through walls, a haunted chorus
with our hoary plumbing? I'm fine with that.
At least you find peace when you're away from me

as I know our son still breathes, one bulbous cheek
smooshed to the mattress, by the way
his wolf yips tremor the monitor.

And some nights I can't sleep without your hands
tumbling the oversized shirt from my shoulders,
or say love without meaning *need*. *Plea.*

Can't close my eyes without smelling harvest dust
you've left on the sheets: sweet and bright as the almond
meat you gather from cracked, green hulls.

FIVE

Dark Matter

It's there:
an itch, unseen
but prickling.

A matter inferred
but unproven

that fills
the gaps
in the night
with seeming.

Hypervelocity Star

I. FLIGHT OF IDEAS

if lack of feeling is a symptom
we call *anhedonia* if chewing
the inside of my cheeks is wrong
I don't want to be wrong

Maggie are peasant skirts
part of the therapist uniform Maggie
I find your bangles distracting
& when you clasp your hands
& tilt your head you look
very much like an interested dog
who also has hands

when the wringing of hands
has become *psychomotor agitation*
blink fifteen times
    but only fifteen

feeling too is a symptom
of a larger illness

the birds of *optimism*
chirp away at the roof
poised for—

II. ANHEDONIA

Lack of *hedonism*, they say,
is the first sign. Without pleasure.
Without desire for pleasure.
The numbing of wonder,
of wander, pleasure
for pleasure's sake excised
and replaced with pink
noise. Without pleasure
is calm. With calmness
even suffering becomes
a kind of pleasure.

III. FAMILY HISTORY

The nights he didn't sleep and didn't need to
my brother picked electronics to bits: removed microphones
from the bag-end of the vacuum cleaner. Blared Zappa,
hosed shattered hard drives off a second-story porch.
But who could be satisfied with the apartment stripped clean
of its monitoring equipment? Who wouldn't wander by day
the rails that slunk through strawberry fields, or itch
to lay a nickel on the tracks, leave your hand there?
Watch it emerge a new object. Flattened by the train,
blurred of its distinctions.

IV. INSOMNIA

At first it's a bad night. A brain
still teeming with the day's mistakes
      awake despite
the body's protestations.
But it keeps
happening:
      fitful glossing
           of the mind, churning

and cocooning of blankets. Clocks insist
on ticking later and later. And it doesn't
get better. Soon the mind
      unfetters   before sleep;
defers dreaming. Limbs leaden by day
      finally stir
           in the evening, muscles
*restless*ly alight
      beneath the skin.

And that persistent dawn keeps
      coming every morning, dragging
           the daylight with it, starting
the whole thing over again.

V. TRIGGER WORDS

Maggie tells me *creativity*
is the sign of an unquiet mind.
Likewise *insomnia*, likewise
hopelessness. Excessive happiness.
Great productivity. No
productivity.

Tonight's Lunar Eclipse shines in your 9th House
of Higher Truth—share the glow
with as many people as possible.
Men, women, birds.
Fuck them all.

Likewise *irritability.*
Likewise *denial.*

VI. GRANDIOSITY

Dear peasants, say
you knew my benevolence.
That I saved you
oxtail, helped myself only
to the barest of marrow.
Allowed you to suck it clean
when I was done.

It's true I've mounted
the cloud cities
and found them wanting—
Laputa, that floating trash vortex—
I have unmade its castle with my breath.

The West Wind said I'm so good at blowing
that he gave up. I'll gust
the hottest dust devils
as stiffly as I please.

VII. EXCESSIVE GUILT

Again, I'll-never-let-him-make-me-small
becomes I-am-a-dot. Feed me sugar
from an eyedropper. My penance: I'll nip
the hangnails from your fingers,
will be unworthy of such an act.

VIII. COMORBIDITY

I might be half a hummingbird,
Maggie. I might be a lot of things.
I do love to tongue the soft insides
of flowers. You could describe me
as nature's hypodermic needle.
That would be fair.

I've known their *torpor*, too.
Have longed to drift from my body
as it lay dormant on the bed.

No. It's not
that I wished to die.
It's that the thought of dying
no longer concerned me.

Or perhaps the woman and the bird
are *comorbid*, comingling.
Don't pretend
you can spot the difference.

IX. PERSEVERATION

reclusive & necrotic I troubled the woodpile
        logs that seemed to stack themselves
                left me blistered
           tore themselves down

I have made life
      inside me once before
          death too
                have spun
                my disorderly threads
     watched them knit themselves
            into sweaters
       into knots
        into arms
   so pale & long
        I could tie them in a bow

the logs
          troubled me
the logs seemed stacked
         against us
against the house
         life's leaded dust
escaped through cracks
         in the plaster
we have become
         the house stacking
& unstacking itself

by the end
     I needed an end
        I could have burned it all
       to the ground

X. DIAGNOSTIC

Does the buzzing of a phone line ever strike you as beautiful?

If, at a party, you stand in a group of five or more people
do their bodies sway in your direction?

Doesn't that dress look amazing on you?

Keeping in mind that you store and filter multitudes, which organ
would you say you resent the most?

Have you noticed a decreased need for sleep?

Do you want to sing?

Tell me about your urges. If I slide my tongue across your foot's
flagrant arch, shudder a breath against it, will I elicit goosebumps?

Would you describe yourself as a risk-taker?

Why not?

Acknowledgements

Thank you to the editors (and readers and entire mastheads) of the following journals in which these poems first appeared:

Bellevue Literary Review: "The Head is a Canvas"
Cincinnati Review: "Endeavour," "Ghazal for Aurora Chasing the Deer," "Kablooey," "Moon Dogs"
Clackamas Literary Review: "Diagnostic," "Family History," "Perseveration"
EPOCH: "The Moon Smells Like Burnt Gunpowder"
failbetter.com: "Ice Plant," "Nautilus"
Goblin Fruit: "Nesting"
Indiana Review: "Sonnet Among the Almond Trees"
Liminality: "Arson Poetica"
PHANTOM: "Discovery"
PN Review: "Emergency Response"
Southern Humanities Review: "Coyote," "Hummingbird Heart"
Spillway: "Guinevere"
The Collagist: "Yellow Window"
THRUSH Poetry Journal: "Anhedonia," "Comorbidity," "Flight of Ideas," "Grandiosity," "Trigger Words"
West Trestle Review: "Scouting"
WomenArts Quarterly Journal: "We Do Not Speak"

"Coma Dreams" and "Pallbearing" were performed onstage by San Francisco's Word for Word Performing Arts Company.
"Coyote," "The Moon Smells Like Burnt Gunpowder" and "Sonnet Among the Almond Trees" were republished by *LitRagger*.
"Coyote" was nominated for a Pushcart Prize by *Southern Humanities Review*.
"Kablooey" was included in the anthology *More Than Soil, More Than Sky: The Modesto Poets*.
"Scouting" was republished in Catenary and nominated for a Pushcart Prize by *West Trestle Review*.

Thank you to judge Sam Witt and the entire Carolina Wren Press team for taking a chance on me.

My gratitude to the Dorothy Sargent Rosenberg Memorial Fund for choosing "Binary Stars," "The Earwig" and "The Wolf at the Door" for their annual poetry prize and to *Southern Humanities Review* for choosing "Coyote" for the Theodore Christian Hoepfner Award for best poem to appear in SHR in 2012.

Thank you to Cornell University for four magical upstate New York winters, an incredible MFA cohort and the start of a poetry career. Thank you to Stanford University for the financial and creative support of the Stegner Fellowship, without which this book would not exist. (Fellow Stegner Fellows, that gratitude extends to you.)

Thank you to all the creative writing professors who whipped me into shape along the way: John Shoptaw, Chris Nealon, Alice Fulton, Ken McClane, Lyrae Van Clief-Stefanon, Ken Fields, Eavan Boland and W.S. DiPiero.

Special thanks to Sarah Scoles, Space Goddess, and to Chiyuma Elliott, Queen of Edits and Grilled Cheese. Thank you, too, to my best friends and first readers: Jack Hollis, Nicole Smith and Robyn Houston. I'd come up with titles for you three, but you know they would be uncouth.

Thank you to justin for 14 years of True Love—marrying you was the single best decision of my life. Thank you to Westley, my burning sun of a son, for introducing me to motherhood, and to Rory, whose mysteries I am only now beginning to unravel.

I'd also like to acknowledge and thank my mother, who didn't live long enough to see me enter high school, let alone write this book. You taught me so much in so few years. Nothing would have been possible without your love.

The text of the book is typeset in 10-point Minion.
The book was designed by Lesley Landis Designs
and printed by BookMobile.